Jaycee's Little Ear

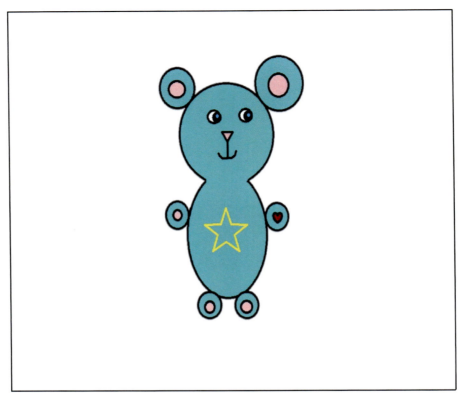

This book is dedicated to my amazing daughter Jaycee
who has Microtia.

ISBN-13: 978-1976103834
ISBN-10: 1976103835

This is Jaycee. She is just waking up to start her school day.
This year Jaycee is in the third grade and loving it!

Jaycee gets out of bed to start the day, the most important part of the day being breakfast.

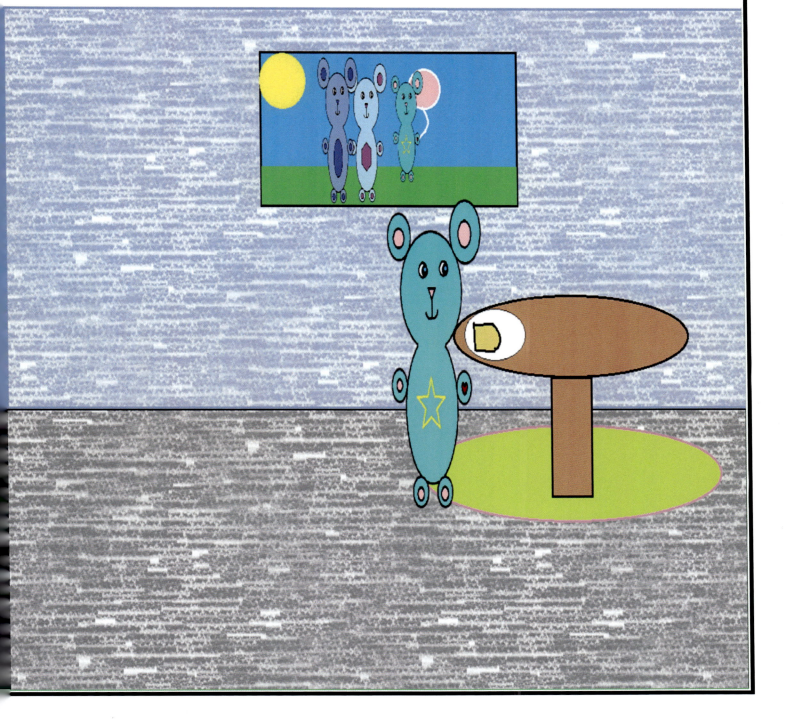

When breakfast is over, Jaycee's Mom reminds her to brush her teeth before school.

There is one thing that is unique about Jaycee that not every other child has. Can you guess what it is?
Jaycee has Microtia, which is a fancy way to say she has one big ear and one small ear.

Jaycee is hard of hearing in her little ear.

She needs to wear a hearing aid to help her hear.

Just like every other child, Jaycee can be a little bit difficult. She does not like wearing her hearing aid until she is in her class.

Every morning Jaycee enjoys the short walk to school with her Mom, Aunt, and cousins.

Jaycee loves her teachers, especially Mr. Tarey. He is a special teacher who helps children who are hard of hearing.
Though sometimes she cannot help wondering why she is the only one in school with a hearing aid.
She just wants to be like every other child.

Later that day Mom picks Jaycee up from school. During the walk home, Jaycee seemed unusually quiet.

"How was your day?" Mom asks with a concerned tone.

"Alright, I just hate being different," Jaycee replies.

"Why would you say that? You are perfect," Mom says while giving Jaycee a warm smile.

"Nobody in my whole school has a little ear, except me," Jaycee replies with a look of sadness.

"You were born unique. I think that makes you special," Mom replies while grabbing ahold of Jaycee's hand.

Jaycee does not reply, remaining silent the rest of the walk home.

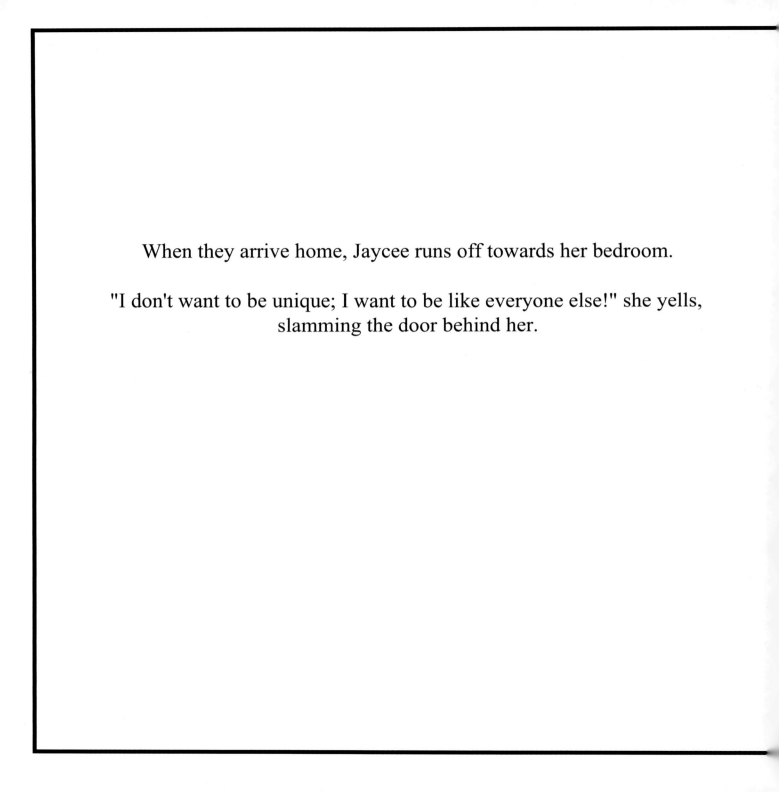

When they arrive home, Jaycee runs off towards her bedroom.

"I don't want to be unique; I want to be like everyone else!" she yells, slamming the door behind her.

Jaycee's parents join her in her bedroom.

"Honey, you are just like every other child," Dad says to Jaycee.

"You just have a little ear, you can do everything any other child can do," Mom says.

What Jaycee's mom said was true. She was like every other child even if she did not realize it.

Jaycee was an excellent soccer player. She enjoyed teaching her cousins how to score a goal.

Jaycee could jump up high, skip, and run around like every other child.

Jaycee could play at the park while enjoying a picnic with her family like any other child.

When Jaycee gets older, she will be able to do anything she wants to do; she could even be an astronaut if she wanted to.

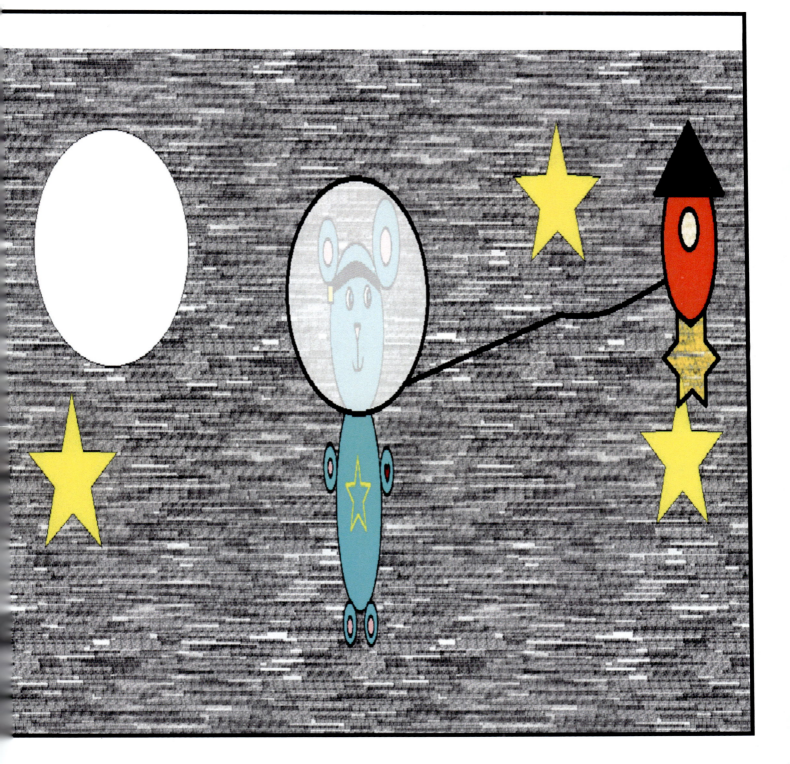

Jaycee finally understood that just because she wears a hearing aid does not mean she isn't like all the other children.

This is a big world full of many types of children. Some of those children even wear hearing aids too.

That is pretty neat!!

The End

Made in the USA
Las Vegas, NV
09 May 2021